DATE DUE

8116

B
ALVER-
EZ

Alverez, Everett.

Everett Alverez, Jr. : a hero for our times.

E.C.I.A. Chapter 2

~~MORNING CREEK ELEMENTARY~~
SAN DIEGO CA 92128

306533 01095 55696A 05756E

EVERETT ALVAREZ, JR.
A Hero for Our Times

EVERETT ALVAREZ, JR.
A Hero for Our Times

By Susan Maloney Clinton

CHILDRENS PRESS ®
CHICAGO

PHOTO CREDITS
Courtesy Alvarez family — 4, 11, 12 (right), 13 (2 photos), 14, 15, 19, 20, 21, 26, 27 (2 photos), 28, 29 (top), 30, 32
AP/Wide World Photos — 1, 17, 18 (2 photos), 22 (bottom left), 24, 25, 29 (bottom)
© Keith Barraclough — Cover
Official U.S. Navy Photograph — 22 (bottom right); by Franklin, 3
UPI/Bettmann Newsphotos — 5, 7, 8, 10, 12 (left), 22 (top)
©*The Washington Post*— 2, 31

Project Editor: E. Russell Primm III
Design: Biner Design
Photo Research: Judy Feldman

Library of Congress Cataloging-in-Publication Data

Clinton, Susan Maloney.
　Everett Alvarez, Jr. : a hero for our time / by Susan Maloney Clinton.
　　p. cm. — (A Picture story biography)
　Summary: An autobiography of the Navy pilot, focusing on his ordeal as the first American prisoner-of-war in North Vietnam.
　ISBN 0-516-04277-7
　1. Alvarez, Everett, 1937- — Juvenile literature. 2. Vietnamese Conflict, 1961-1975—Prisoners and prisons, North Vietnamese—Juvenile literature. 3. Prisoners of war—United States—Biography—Juvenile literature. 4. Prisoners of war—Vietnam—Biography—Juvenile literature. [1. Alvarez, Everett, 1937- . 2. Prisoners of war. 3. Vietnamese Conflict, 1961-1975—Prisoners and prisons, North Vietnamese.] I. Clinton, Susan. II. Title. III. Series
DS559.4.A484 1990
959.704'37—dc20
[B]
[92]　　　　　　　　　　　　　　　　　　　　　　　　　　　　　90-38375
　　　　　　　　　　　　　　　　　　　　　　　　　　　　　　　　CIP
　　　　　　　　　　　　　　　　　　　　　　　　　　　　　　　　AC

Copyright © 1990 by Childrens Press ®, Inc.
All rights reserved. Published simultaneously in Canada.
Printed in the United States of America.
1 2 3 4 5 6 7 8 9 10 R 99 98 97 96 95 94 93 92 91 90

Navy pilot Everett Alvarez, Jr., guided his fighter-bomber toward the coast of North Vietnam. This was a bombing mission—his first. When he heard, "Okay boys, let's give her the gun," he started to dive. The plane zoomed down at 500 miles an hour. Alvarez was looking for enemy boats. He saw four of them and fired. He also saw that the Vietnamese were firing back.

A Skyhawk fighter-bomber like the one Everett Alvarez, Jr., flew in Vietnam.

Seconds later, Everett's plane shook and filled with smoke. He was hit! Alvarez pulled a ring and a rocket fired him, seat and all, out of the cockpit. His parachute opened, and he drifted down slowly into the water. From the bay, he watched the last American plane fly away.

Vietnamese fishermen in a small boat aimed their rifles at Everett, pulled him into the boat, and tied him up. He couldn't understand their language, but he could tell the fishermen were very angry. He had no idea what the Vietnamese would do with him, or where they would take him.

The United States and North Vietnam were not at war, but they were awfully close to it. The two nations were struggling over the control of South Vietnam. There had not yet

U.S. President Lyndon B. Johnson

been any direct fighting between North Vietnam and the United States, not until August 4, 1964.

That night, two U.S. ships called for help. They believed that North Vietnamese boats were attacking them. Everett Alvarez was one of the pilots who flew in to help them. In the darkness, however, he couldn't see any enemy boats. Neither could any of the other pilots.

U.S. President Lyndon B. Johnson was angry. He believed the North

Vietnamese were attacking American ships. The next day, on August 5, 1964, he ordered U.S. planes to make the first bombing raid on North Vietnam. On that mission Everett Alvarez, Jr., was shot down—and became the first American prisoner-of-war in North Vietnam.

A North Vietnamese sailor escorts Everett Alvarez to prison after he was shot down in August 1964.

Everett Alvarez was moved from place to place. He always hoped, however, that American officials would come and take him home. No one came. Instead, Everett was taken to a prison in Hanoi, the capital of North Vietnam.

Guards gave him a baggy pair of pants and a shirt. They took him to a room with a narrow bed with boards for a mattress. For a toilet, he had a rusty bucket. For a sink, there was a vat of cold water covered with moss and big cockroaches. The room was lit with one light bulb that burned all day and all night. In the low light, Everett could see the rats run across his room at night. This room would be his home for an entire year.

There was no one to talk to and nothing to do. The guard brought food

The North Vietnamese held many of the American POWs in Ly Nam de Prison, better known as the "Hanoi Hilton."

that was barely eatable. One day Everett got a pig's hoof floating in dirty gravy. Some days a whole blackbird, feathers and all, would lie on his plate. Alvarez was slowly starving. He began to think he would not live to go home.

To fill the time, Everett relived in his mind scenes from home. He remembered his first ride in an open-cockpit airplane. He thought about his Navy training. At twenty-two, he had joined the Navy to train as a pilot.

Everett Alvarez, Jr., in uniform, 1963.

Alvarez drew strength from thinking about his family. His grandparents had come to the United States from Mexico. They worked hard as they moved from one railroad camp to another. Everett's grandmother, MaMona, kept the family together. Everett had inherited his grandmother's strong spirit.

Everett's parents, too, had always worked hard. His father, Lalo, was a metal welder in a factory. His mother,

Everett's parents, Lalo and Chloe Alvarez, (left), and Everett at age 2 1/2 (right).

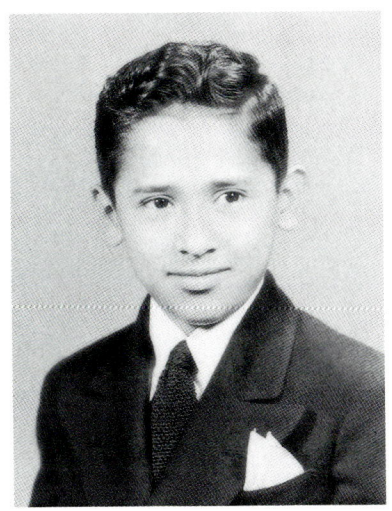

Everett at the time of his first communion (above), and a family portrait (right).

also worked in a factory canning fruits and vegetables. Everett was born in 1937. For much of his life, he and his family lived in a small house in Salinas, California. After sixth grade, Everett spent his summers doing field work to earn money for school clothes.

Everett's parents wanted him to understand that he would have to earn the things he wanted in life. Neither of his parents had been able to finish high school. Both Lalo and Chloe wanted Everett to have a good education. Everett followed their advice. In high school, he took extra courses in science and math so that he could go to college. When Everett graduated from the University of Santa Clara, his

Everett Alvarez's junior high school basketball team. Everett is in the lower row, first from left.

Everett tying for first place during a high school track meet.

parents were very proud. These memories helped Everett during his days in prison.

Praying helped, too. Everett's strong belief in God made him feel less alone. One of the first things Everett did after his capture was scratch a cross onto the wall of his room. He often stood before the cross and repeated the prayers he had learned as a young boy.

After six weeks of awful food, the jailers saw that Everett would die soon without good food. One day they began sending him better meals with bread, eggs, and once in a while, fruit. The Vietnamese had shown that they had absolute power. But, Everett had shown them that he could undergo terrible hardships.

Alvarez didn't see other Americans for the first year. Then, one day, he was moved to a prison with other U.S. soldiers. They invented a secret code so that they could communicate without the Vietnamese knowing what they said. They tapped the code letters on the walls of their cells.

Altogether, during the nine years of open war between the North Vietnamese and the United States, 500 American pilots were captured. The North Vietnamese held the pilots in several different prisons. The pilots were treated like criminals, and the news media in North Vietnam made the people hate the Americans.

In June 1966, Everett and a group of POWs were taken into Hanoi. They were made to walk among a crowd of angry people. For an hour, the people threw stones at the POWs, kicked them, and beat them with sticks and fists.

The POWs had to make important decisions. They decided that no one

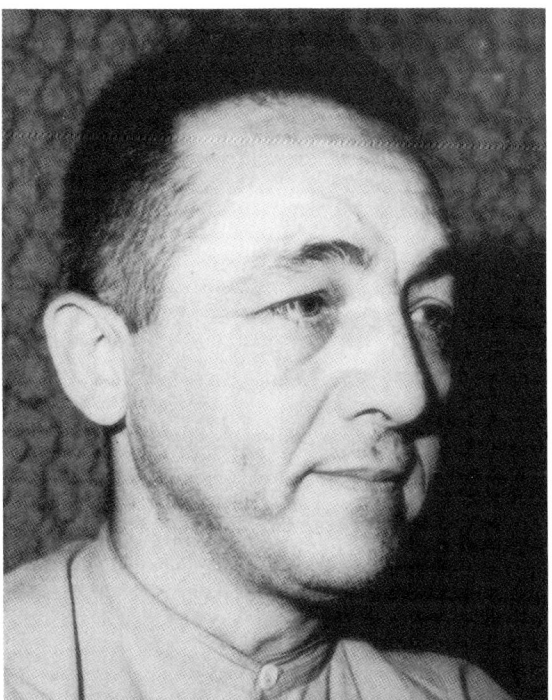

A fellow officer, Lt. Col. Robinson Risner, was led with Everett Alvarez and other POWs through angry crowds in the streets of Hanoi.

Jerry Coffee (left) and Dave Carey (right) became close friends with Everett during his time in prison.

should accept any offer of freedom until all of them were free to go home. If they all stuck together, the Vietnamese would not be able to use them against one another. This togetherness became very important.

From the summer of 1966 until the fall of 1969, life in the prison camp became harder and more brutal than before. Food was cut back. For many months they ate nothing but rice. The guards let the food sit on the ground so that the rice was covered with ants and roaches.

Some of the POWs died from mistreatment during these years. Many got permanent injuries. The president of North Vietnam, Ho Chi Minh, died in September 1969. The guards finally let up, and life improved for the POWs. They got better food. They had more chances to exercise outside, and they were allowed to gather in groups of 20. Everett became close friends with two of his cellmates, Jerry Coffee and Dave Carey.

In 1972, the POWs in Hanoi were allowed to gather together on Christmas Day to sing carols.

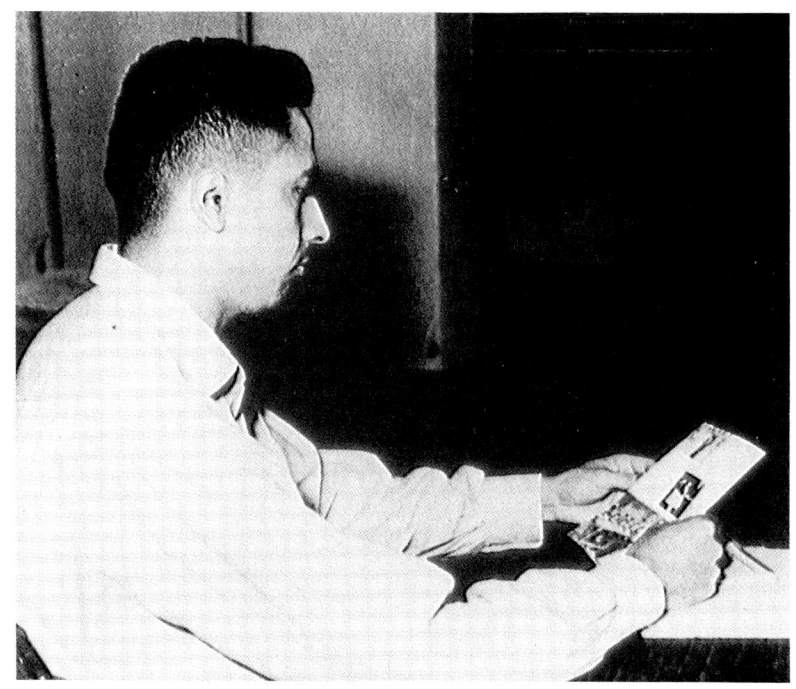
Everett was allowed to receive only one or two letters each year that he was held captive.

For two years, Everett had not received any letters from his wife. Finally, on Christmas Day, 1971, a letter from his mother told him that his wife had not waited for him to come home. She had divorced him and married another man. This news made him very sad, but he knew that he could not give in.

The POWs learned that the United States and North Vietnam were trying to make peace. Everett and the other POWs were told that they could be going home. Years of waiting and disappointment had taught the POWs to wait. But peace had been made, and Everett Alvarez flew home to California on February 16, 1973. He was the first POW off the plane, and he gave a speech on behalf of all the former prisoners.

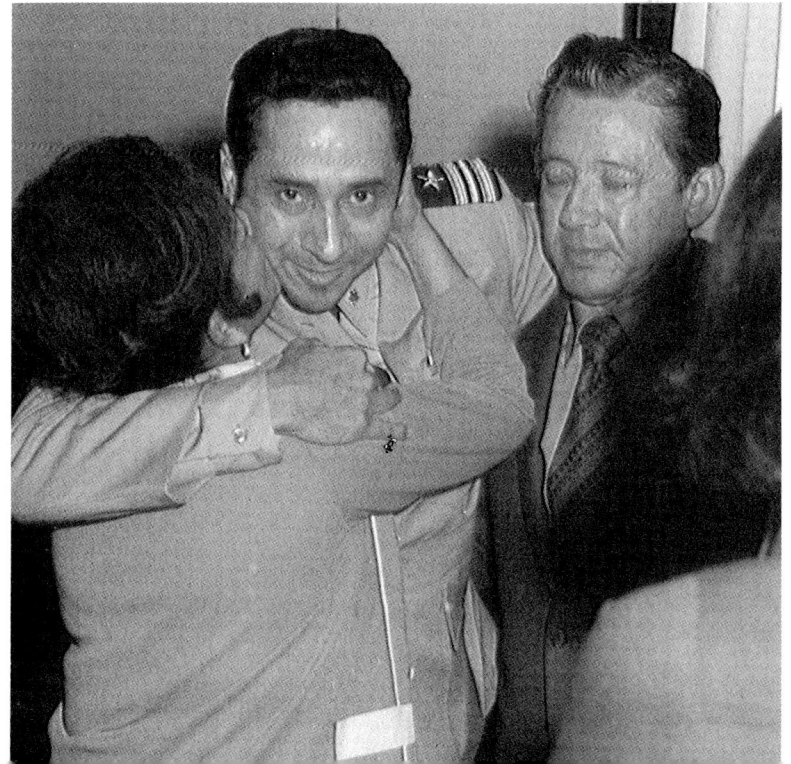

Everett Alvarez, Jr., was finally reunited with his family in February 1973.

In March 1973, Everett's home town, Santa Clara, California, held a parade in his honor (left). Before his return to the U.S., Everett rested in a air base hospital in the Philippines (bottom left). The Alvarez family after Everett's return to the U.S. (bottom right).

Everett Alvarez came home a hero. A crowd of 100,000 people came to his welcome-home parade in Santa Clara, California. People all over the country wrote to him; hundreds of groups invited him to speak. On one of his trips, he met Tammy Ilyas. When President Nixon gave a White House party for all the returned POWs, Tammy was Everett's date. The two were married on October 27, 1973.

The Navy honored Alvarez with medals for his bravery and endurance—the Silver Star, two Purple Hearts, two Legions of Merit, and others. Even though Everett could have spent all his time speaking about his time in Vietnam, that wasn't what he wanted.

Alvarez stayed in the Navy and studied computers. When he finished a

Everett and his wife-to-be, Tammy Ilyas, during a dinner at the White House given by President Richard Nixon.

master's degree, the Navy gave him the job of helping to design a new and better fighter-bomber. Alvarez also started going to law school at night.

In 1980, at 42 years old, Commander Alvarez retired from the Navy. In the spring of 1981, he received a new job from President Ronald Reagan. The president wanted

Everett to help run the Peace Corps. The Peace Corps had 5,000 young Americans working in 60 different countries. For a year, he traveled all over the world, visiting Peace Corps workers and talking to the leaders of foreign countries.

When he came home, Alvarez had another job offer. This time President Reagan asked him to help run the Veterans Administration (VA). The VA works with all the people who have

Everett and Tammy Alvarez on their wedding day, October 27, 1973.

Everett Alvarez, second from right, and U.S. senators during hearings on his appointment to the Veterans Administration.

been in the United States military. Part of Alvarez's job was to meet with veterans and find ways to solve their problems. Veterans respected him because they knew Everett understood their experiences.

On November 13, 1982, the United States honored all the veterans of the

Vietnam Conflict with a new monument made of black granite and shaped like a "v". Carved in this stone wall are the names of nearly 58,000 men and women who died in Vietnam. People gathered from all over the country for the dedication of the monument.

At left, Everett Alvarez stands in his office at the Veterans Administration. Part of his job was to meet with veterans from the various wars that the United States had fought.

Everett Alvarez was asked to speak at the ceremony. He told the crowd that the wall was a tribute to all the people who served their country in Southeast Asia. He also said that the wall would keep alive the memory of all those who did not return from the war.

For four years, Alvarez helped run the VA's hospitals and the computers that held the medical records. Part of his job was to meet once a month with

Everett Alvarez, Jr., was chosen to speak for the Veterans Administration at the dedication of the Vietnam Veterans Memorial in 1982.

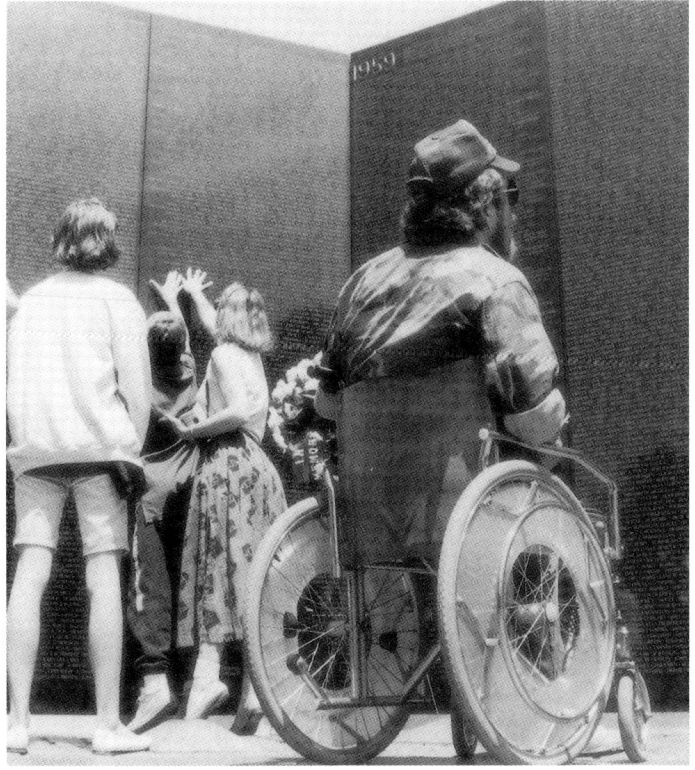

A huge crowd of people attended the dedication ceremony for the Vietnam Veterans Memorial (above). The wall contains the names of all those who were killed in the Vietnam Conflict (right).

President Ronald Reagan honored Everett Alvarez, Jr., with a POW medal in 1988.

President Reagan. He also had to explain the Veterans Administration's needs to the Congress.

Today, Everett Alvarez is the president of his own company. His business combines two areas that he knows very well. He helps different parts of the government set up computer systems. He also still helps the president of the United States from time to time. President George Bush asked Everett to help plan for an international meeting in July 1990. At this meeting, leaders of seven nations met to talk about trade among their countries.

Alvarez also spends a lot of time enjoying his family life. He and his wife, Tammy, have two sons. Marc was born in 1974, and Bryan was born in 1976. Everett never wants his sons to go through an experience such as his. He does, however, want them to have the self-confidence, faith, strength, and endurance that have made him both a national hero and leader.

A recent photo of the Alvarez family.

EVERETT ALVAREZ, JR.

1937	Everett Alvarez, Jr., born in Salinas, California
1955	Tie for High School League track championship
1960	Joined the Navy and trained as a fighter pilot
1964	August 5—First POW taken by the North Vietnamese during the Vietnam Conflict
1966	Everett Alvarez and a group of POWs were moved into a prison in Hanoi, North Vietnam
1973	February 16—Released from prison and reunited with family in California; October 27—Married Tammy Ilyas in Pittsburgh, PA
1980	Retired from U.S. Navy
1981	Appointed to Peace Corps by President Ronald Reagan
1982	Appointed Deputy Administrator for the Veterans Administration by President Ronald Reagan
1982	Dedicated Vietnam Veterans Memorial in Washington, DC
1988	Received POW medal from President Ronald Reagan
1990	Advisor to President George Bush for the 1990 Economic Summit

INDEX

Alvarez, Bryan (son), 31
Alvarez, Chloe (mother), 12-13, 14
Alvarez, Lalo (father), 12, 14
Alvarez, Marc (son), 31
awards, 23
Bush, George, 30
childhood, 11
Carey, Dave, 19
Coffee, Jerry, 19
Economic Summit, 30-31
grandparents, 12,

Hanoi, North Vietnam, 9, 17
Ho Chi Minh, 19
home-coming parade, 23
Ilyas, Tammy (Mrs. Everett Alvarez), 23, 31
Johnson, Lyndon B., 7
Legion of Merit, 23
Nixon, Richard M., 23
North Vietnam, 5, 17, 19
peace agreement, 21
Peace Corps, 25
prison conditions, 9-10, 18, 19

Purple Heart, 23
Reagan, Ronald, 24, 25, 30
release from prison, 21
Salinas, California, 13
Silver Star, 23
University of Santa Clara, 14
Veterans Administration (VA), 25-26
Vietnam Veterans Memorial, 26-28
Vietnam war, 6-7, 8

ABOUT THE AUTHOR

Susan Maloney Clinton holds a Ph.D. in English and is a part-time teacher of English Literature at Northwestern University in Evanston, Illinois. Her articles have appeared in such publications as *Consumer's Digest*, *Family Style Magazine*, and the Chicago *Reader*. In addition, she has contributed biographical and historical articles to *Encyclopaedia Britannica* and *Compton's Encyclopedia*, and has written reader stories and other materials for a number of educational publishers. Ms. Clinton lives in Chicago with her husband, Pat, and their two sons.